Exploring Japanese Mythology

Don Nardo

ReferencePoint Press

San Diego, CA

Printed in the United States

For more information, contact:
ReferencePoint Press, Inc.
PO Box 27779
San Diego, CA 92198
www.ReferencePointPress.com

LIBRARY OF CONGRESS CATALOGING-IN-PUBLICATION DATA

Names: Nardo, Don, 1947- author
Title: Exploring Japanese mythology / by Don Nardo.
Description: San Diego, CA : ReferencePoint Press, Inc., 2026. | Includes bibliographical references and index.
Identifiers: LCCN 2025005152 (print) | LCCN 2025005153 (ebook) | ISBN 9781678210748 library binding | ISBN 9781678210755 ebook
Subjects: LCSH: Mythology, Japanese--Juvenile literature
Classification: LCC BL2202.3 .N37 2026 (print) | LCC BL2202.3 (ebook) | DDC 398.20952--dc23/eng/20250319
LC record available at https://lccn.loc.gov/2025005152
LC ebook record available at https://lccn.loc.gov/2025005153

The Phantom's Secret

Long, long ago, in a small town in southern Japan, a beautiful young woman named Osono married a successful merchant named Nagaraya. They were happy together and had a son. Unfortunately for the boy and his father, Osono fell ill and died in the fourth year of the marriage, and members of both families grieved deeply.

It was on the day following the funeral that something strange occurred. Osono and Nagaraya's son told some gathered relatives that he had just seen his mother in her bedchamber. At first they naturally thought he was mistaken. But then they went to that room and saw for themselves that Osono's spirit was indeed standing in plain sight beside her favorite chest of drawers. As described by the late Greco-American translator and storyteller Patrick L. Hearn, "Her head and shoulders could be very distinctly seen; but from the waist downwards the figure thinned into invisibility. It was like an imperfect reflection of her, and transparent as a shadow on water."[1]

Osono

A wife and mother who dies young and whose spirit returns to retrieve a secret hidden in her home

The relatives met and tried to figure out why Osono's spirit was visiting the house. Initially, they concluded that perhaps it upset her that her belongings in the drawers had not yet been donated to the local religious temple, per social custom. So they emptied the drawers and gave the items to the temple.

Osono's spirit did not go away, however. It still stood, staring intently at the now empty bureau. Seriously worried, Nagaraya's mother went to the temple and told its head priest what was happening. He suggested that there must still be something in the drawers that was worrying the woman's spirit and keeping it from proceeding to the afterlife. He offered to go to the bedchamber and keep watch.

True to his word, the priest kept vigil that night in the bedchamber. At a bit past midnight, Osono's spirit appeared once more, and the priest politely addressed it. He asked whether there was something left in the bureau that was upsetting her, and the apparition gently nodded its head. Although carefully searching the drawers, the priest found nothing. And then it occurred to him that there might be something hidden beneath the paper lining the bottoms of the drawers. Sure enough, he soon found a letter. He could tell from the expression on Osono's face that this was indeed the object of her distress. He saw that it was a love letter written to her by a young man a few months before she had married Nagaraya.

"Shall I burn it for you?"[2] the priest asked. And the phantom nodded once again. Minutes later, the letter was no more, and Osono's spirit vanished, never to return. The priest informed the family that all was now well and that Osono had finally moved on. He did not mention the letter. It was a secret he took to his grave.

Two Thematic Threads

This charming story, well known and frequently recited in Japan, combines two of the most prominent thematic threads that run throughout the numerous tales making up Japanese mythology. One is a powerful respect for the dead. Historian Daniel Kershaw calls it "a deep reverence and veneration of the dead, not only the heroic figures in Japanese history and myth but also each family's ancestral dead as well."[3] In Osono's tale, that theme is illustrated by the family's attempts to appease her spirit, as well as by the priest's keeping of her secret.

The second prominent theme manifest in this and other stories is the characters' strong sense of morality. The events of the story suggest that Osono felt it would be unethical to leave the letter behind; clearly, the discovery that she loved another man besides her husband might be overly distressing for both her son and his father. And she wants to spare them that upset.

This sentiment is not unusual, because for many centuries there has been a strong sense of ethics among the bulk of Japan's population. And the idea that human interactions inevitably have moral consequences runs throughout the Japanese myths. Most modern scholars think this derives from the influence of Confucianism,

Confucius was a philosopher whose idea that human interactions inevitably have moral consequences runs throughout Japanese myths.

which entered Japan from China in the sixth century CE. Confucian philosophy is often summed up by the so-called Golden Rule, the maxim that holds that people should treat others the way they would like to be treated. Even today, moral principles based on Confucianism are taught in Japanese schools. These include "themes such as courtesy, consideration, friendship, [and] modesty,"[4] says the Tokyo-based online newspaper Japan Today. Therefore, it is not surprising that ethical concepts abound in the Japanese myths.

Confucianism

A philosophy that teaches that people can achieve good moral character in part by treating others in the same way that they prefer to be treated

The Importance of Keeping a Promise

One of the most famous of all the Japanese tales—"The Grateful Crane"—contains such a moral. In one of the several existing versions, an elderly man finds a crane caught in a trap in the woods. He frees the beautiful bird, which flies away. The next day a beautiful young woman arrives at his door and offers to cook and clean for him. She does so and makes a stunning-looking piece of fabric for him. He asks her to make another one, but she makes him promise not to peek into the room where she will be working the loom.

The man cannot resist peeking, however, and when he does, he sees the crane he saved running the loom; it yanks out its own feathers to use in making the cloth. Realizing that the man broke his promise, the crane, which had been helping him out of gratitude, leaves forever. Japanese parents often tell this story to their children to teach them the importance of keeping a promise when they make one. It is one of the many life lessons found in the diverse and fascinating treasury of Japanese myths.

The Creation of the World and Japan

Long ago, in a mostly forgotten age before the world existed, there was nothing but chaos. Particles of all sizes and shapes, made up of random elements, floated here and there, sometimes colliding, and there was no order to anything in existence. Over time, however, the lighter particles floated upward, forming the sacred High Plain of Heaven. At the same time, the heavier particles sank downward and became the earth. The land was gelatinous and still formless, like a jellyfish, and the sea was vast and seemingly endlessly deep.

Then, rather suddenly, the first *kami*, or deities, appeared from the prehistoric ooze. There were five of these initial gods, who were invisible, genderless, nameless, and had no defined shapes. From them came seven subsequent generations of kami. All their members, except for the last two, were also invisible and formless, with no mates.

Those last two kami changed everything. Not only were they visible, they also had solid, humanlike form, consisting of a head, a torso, two arms, and two legs. They also had genders and names. The male was called Izanagi, while the female's name was Izanami. And only moments after springing into existence, they heard their many kami ancestors crying out together. All the earlier, invisible deities urged Izanagi and Izanami to create solid landforms in the sea. Those islands, all the gods predicted, would later become the greatest of all nations, the wondrous Japan.

And so, Izanagi and Izanami proceeded with the creation of the Japanese archipelago in the ocean-covered earth. First, the two divine beings built a bridge—a sort of stairway—connected to the High Plain of Heaven to give themselves something solid to stand on. Then they seized hold of the magnificent Jeweled Spear, or Tenkei, a magical artifact the earlier kami had somehow conjured up for them. According to the *Kojiki*, Japan's first sacred book, Izanagi and Izanami stood "upon the Floating Bridge of Heaven, pushed down the Jeweled Spear and stirred [the ocean] with it, whereupon, when they

Tenkei

The special spear used by the creator gods Izanagi and Izanami to make the first Japanese island

Izanagi and Izanami (shown) were urged by their divine ancestors to create solid landforms in the sea. Those islands would later become Japan.

had stirred the brine till it curdled, and drew the spear up, the brine that dripped down from the end of the spear was piled up and became the island. This is the Island of Onogoro."[5]

After building a palace for themselves on the small isle of Onogoro, Izanagi and Izanami created the other, larger Japanese islands, including, among hundreds of others, Honshu, Awaji, Oki, Iki, Shikoku, and Kyushu. The lands became the home to a race of nondivine, mortal creatures called humans, who physically looked like the two creator deities. The origins of those early, lowly people remain largely unknown and were not attributed to the gods. This concluded the first of Japanese mythology's three main stages of the creation.

The Basis for Japan's Creation Myths

These events, including the formation of both the early gods and the Japanese islands, are described in the *Kojiki*. Roughly translating as "Record of Ancient Things," it is Japan's earliest known book, as well as a major text of Shinto, Japan's indigenous, or native, religion. By extension, it is also the basis for the several Japanese creation myths.

Attempts to Locate Heaven

Shortly after Amaterasu's creation, the other kami agreed that she should take charge of Takamagahara, the High Plain of Heaven. The *Kojiki* and other early Japanese mythological writings did not precisely define or describe that heavenly abode. Nor did they say exactly where it was. As a result, over the centuries various Japanese scholars and other writers have offered their own descriptions of that sacred place. In ancient, medieval, and early modern times, the most widely accepted view was that heaven existed in the sky, high above earth's surface. However, other, less popular views surfaced from time to time. One seventeenth-century Confucian scholar suggested that Takamagahara lay in Japan's Hitachi Province; later theories posited that heaven was located somewhere in South Korea. Since the end of World War II in 1945, however, most educated Japanese have accepted that if heaven does exist, it is a mystical plane of existence that humans will never be able to precisely locate or define.

A court scholar named Ono Yasumaro wrote the Kojiki*, which is Japan's earliest known book and the basis for several creation myths.*

A polytheistic faith, Shinto revolves around the numerous supernatural kami, thought to inhabit all things, including trees, lakes, mountains, and nature's various forces. It was these beings that the *Kojiki*'s author, a court scholar named Ono Yasumaro, had in mind when he penned that work in about 712 CE. He wanted to show that Japan's rulers were directly descended from the early Shinto gods. Yasumaro sought to demonstrate a clear line of descent from the sun goddess, Amaterasu (who appears in the creation story's third stage), to Japan's emperor. Using myths as a political tool, therefore, the *Kojiki* established that the emperors were semidivine.

Whether or not the emperors were descended from gods, inarguably those rulers' subjects were ordinary mortals. And modern historians and mythologists find it odd that the *Kojiki* does not address human origins. That is "something that we usually find in all other creation myths around the world," says Marky Star, an expert on Japanese history and culture. "Why would that be overlooked or left out?" he asks. No one knows for sure, he points out. But he suggests that perhaps in ancient Japanese eyes, the existence of humans "may have been self-evident. Humans were just part of the natural word, no different from birds, snakes, and fish." So it might be that "they required no creation explanation."[6]

Establishing Male Dominance in Society

Far less ambiguous are the events of the second stage of the Japanese creation stories and their influences on early Japanese society. Those narratives deal mainly with the personal interactions between the creator deities Izanagi and Izanami. At Izanami's suggestion, the two got married and began producing numerous kami offspring.

Although the two were initially excited about having children, they were sorely disappointed by their first child. Terribly malformed, the baby, whom they named Hiruko, had neither arms nor legs. Not knowing what else to do, with great sadness the parents carefully wrapped the small body in swaddling clothes and set it adrift in a basket in the ocean. They never saw the child again.

Izanagi and Izanami naturally wanted to know why their first baby had been born so badly deformed. So they held a conference with most of the older kami, who discussed the matter at length. After deliberating, those gods said they had found the problem. "It was inappropriate," they explained (as Star tells it), "for a woman to begin matrimonial bonds and initiate sex. The male should do all of that first."[7]

The kami said that the two creators should try again, this time with Izanagi approaching his wife instead of the other way around. Sure enough, thereafter, using that approach, the couple was able to beget perfectly formed children. For ancient Japanese society, this myth seemed to justify male dominance and female submissiveness. After all, the argument went, male superiority had long ago been ordained by the gods themselves.

The Boundary Between the Living and the Dead

With the social hierarchy in place, the couple went on to conceive several more kami, among them Ebisu, god of prosperity and good fortune. Unfortunately for Izanami, while giving birth to the fire god, Kagutsuchi, she was badly burned and died.

Not surprisingly, Izanagi was devastated by his wife's passing. It heartened him somewhat that although her body had expired, her spirit lived on. Yet it grieved him that her soul now resided in the dark, damp, filthy underworld called Yomi. He hurried there, hoping to retrieve her spirit, but when he arrived, he heard that she had already eaten some of that subterranean realm's plants, and that made it impossible for her to leave.

The distraught Izanagi refused to accept that his mate was stuck in that awful place forever, so he searched relentlessly till he found her. To his horror, however, he saw that her spirit still inhabited her rotting corpse, and in Japanese myth, seeing a decaying body made the viewer ritually impure. In a state of panic, Izanagi turned his back on his wife and ran. Feeling

Amaterasu and the Japanese Emperors

According to Japan's creation stories and some key subsequent myths, the first emperor of that land, Jimmu, had a direct ancestral link to the sun goddess, Amaterasu. Indeed, those tales claim that he was that deity's great-grandson. Hence, he (and by extension later emperors related to him) was semidivine, or at least specially chosen to rule by Amaterasu herself. As late as the early twentieth century, large numbers of Japanese believed that Jimmu had been a real historical figure; they accepted the legends saying he had ruled from 660 to 585 BCE and that at the time of his death he was 160 or even older. Through the mid-twentieth century, many Japanese still clung to the idea that their existing emperor was descended directly from Amaterasu and therefore at least partly a god. After Japan's defeat in World War II, however, the emperor, Hirohito, was compelled to renounce his claim to divinity. Today Japanese historians accept that Jimmu was strictly a mythical individual, and most Japanese see the emperor as a highly respected symbol of national unity and morality, but quite mortal rather than partly divine.

betrayed, Izanami gathered a small army of decaying hags and zombies. She also called forth Fujin, a green-skinned child she had birthed in Yomi. Together, Izanami, Fujin, and the hags and zombies dashed after her fleeing husband in what became a long, frantic pursuit. During that chase, writes University of Oklahoma scholar Joshua Frydman, "three times Izanagi removes accessories from his person—his hair tie, his comb, and finally his sword—and throws them behind him. Each one turns into a distraction to keep Izanami's army from reaching him. Finally, Izanagi reaches the . . . entrance to [Yomi], and after passing it, he blocks it with a giant boulder."[8]

After his escape from the underworld, Izanagi spoke to Izanami through a crack in one side of the boulder. They agreed that their marriage was now dissolved. Furthermore, he would continue with the creation, while she would now become the queen of Yomi and oversee that dismal land of dead souls. This myth proved to be important to the ancient Japanese because in their eyes it contained a believable explanation for what happened to humans after they died. Their spirits went to a gloomy abode ruled by a former creator goddess. Although decidedly unpleasant, it was not a place of retribution and punishment, like the Christian hell, but simply another plane of existence.

The Gods of the Natural World

The third major stage of the Japanese creation myths begins with Izanagi dealing with the fact that he had become impure while in Yomi. To purify himself, he conducted a Shinto ritual called *misogi*. It consists of scrubbing the entire body, sometimes accompanied by saying prayers, doing certain exercises, and throwing handfuls of salt.

It was while undergoing misogi that Izanagi noticed something strange. As he methodically scrubbed himself, small pieces of his skin fell off onto the ground and before his astounded eyes gyrated, expanded, and swiftly grew into living beings. It soon became clear that he was once more creating new kami, this time from his own cells. This went on for hours, until finally he gave rise to what later generations of Japanese would call the Three Precious Children. The most prominent and revered gods of Japanese Shinto mythology, they were the radiant sun goddess Amaterasu; Tsukuyomi, who would later become the moon god; and Susanoo, often described as a deity who could control powerful natural forces.

Sun goddess Amaterasu is well known in Japanese Shinto mythology. She is pictured with Tsukuyomi and Susanoo.

Tsukuyomi
The god who oversees the night and the moon

Looking upon these splendid divinities, Izanagi was enormously content. As Frydman tells it, he appointed "them as his heirs over all the natural world that he and Izanami had created. Amaterasu [was] granted rulership over the High Plain of Heaven."[9] Although impressive in their own right, Tsukuyomi and Susanoo, along with the rest of the kami, ever after remained subservient to the sun goddess.

Completing Creation and Ensuring Continual Life

Despite the rise to prominence of the majestic Three Precious Children, it quickly became clear that the creation and its mission to bring a precise order to the world was not yet complete. For one thing, Tsukuyomi initially lacked distinct duties within nature and shared the daytime with his sister deity, Amaterasu. Also, no fertile farmlands yet existed on the Japanese islands, so the food that both the kami and humans ate was, as a temporary measure, made by a goddess named Ukemochi. She magically manufactured it inside her body and squeezed it out through her mouth and anus.

Ukemochi
A goddess who made food until Tsukuyomi slew her

All of this changed after Tsukuyomi discovered how the food was made. Afraid that eating what came from Ukemochi's anus might be impure, in a fit of rage he killed her. Hearing about this crime, Amaterasu, the most powerful of all the kami, banished Tsukuyomi permanently to a place without her light. It became known as the night, which thereafter remained separate from the day. And in that darkness Tsukuyomi became the god of the only light-emitting object in that sphere—the moon.

That left unsolved the problem of the lack of fertile soil on the islands. There was no way to grow crops, and with Ukemochi gone, there was no food being produced. The solution to this problem came from one of Susanoo's offspring, a young god named Onamuji. He was known for his kindness and desire to help the relatively few humans and animals living in Japan. After convincing the other kami that he was competent to tackle the food crisis, he became known as Okuninushi, the "Great Land Master." With the aid of an assistant named Sukunabikona, he made the land and soils of Japan ready for large-scale cultivation. This prepared the way for humans to feed themselves and multiply, and in this way the compassionate Okuninushi completed the great cycle of creation begun years before by Izanagi and Izanami. Now life could continue on the great islands.

Tales of the Gods and Goddesses

The creator gods Izanagi and Izanami were terribly sad that their first child, Hiruko, had been born without arms and legs. They had no idea how to raise a baby who would face so many hardships. Yet they could not bring themselves to do what some older kami suggested—kill the infant and spare him that difficult future. So Hiruko's parents reluctantly placed him in a basket made of reeds and set that vessel adrift in the sea.

As it turned out, young Hiruko had a far brighter future ahead of him than anyone could have imagined. The basket carrying the infant god floated for an unknown number of days, until it reached a point near the eastern shore of Hokkaido, a large island situated in northern Japan. There, some sea creatures saw the child and told their master about it. He was none other than Ryujin, a powerful water deity, who normally looked like a dragon but who sometimes shape-shifted into human form. Known for his kindness, the Dragon King, as he was sometimes called, made sure that the people on nearby shores had plenty of seafood to eat. And because of this, he was widely seen as a friend and protector of fishers.

Ryujin
A powerful Japanese water god who helped the abandoned kami Hiruko

Ryujin also possessed various mysterious healing powers. And after taking pity on the orphaned Hiruko, he used those abilities to make the child grow arms and legs. By the time the youngster was three, he could walk, and at age five he could run and play with human children.

Furthermore, when the boy was somewhat older, Ryujin revealed to him that his parents were gods, which meant that Hiruko was also divine and had supernatural powers. The question was how the young man would choose to use those abilities. And the Dragon King was delighted when Hiruko announced that he would devote himself to helping others, both humans and kami

Water deity Ryujin in the form of a dragon, along with his sea minions, chases a pearl diver who stole his jewels.

alike. In the words of historian Gregory Wright, "Eternally grateful for the generosity and luck that had saved his life, Hiruko—now calling himself Ebisu—began spreading joy and luck to all he encountered. Having never lost his affinity for the sea, Ebisu was always sure to look favorably upon fishermen."[10]

Two Sacred Pantheons

One reason that this myth about Hiruko's upbringing and fate has long been popular in Japan is that it tells how two important gods—Ebisu and Ryujin—met and interacted in ways beneficial to humans. Like many other Japanese deities, both are Shinto kami. In very general terms, the term *kami* is often defined as "nature god." Michael Ashkenazi, an expert on Japanese religion and culture, explains that a kami is "a powerful being with an interest in the lives of humans and the ability to intervene in human affairs, either directly or indirectly, by influencing the activities of other kami, animals, or natural events and features: in short, a deity."[11]

Considering that Shinto was Japan's primary religion for many centuries, it is not surprising that Shinto kami proliferated throughout the Japanese islands. It became common to say that there were 8 million kami in all. But that is meant as a figure of speech rather than a literal fact. Saying there are millions of those deities simply means that they are too numerous for an average person to count. Most kami are nameless, and each oversees some small facet of nature, such as a specific mountain, lake, or river. In contrast, the far fewer named kami are powerful enough to affect all of humanity or nature in general. Besides Ebisu, the god of good luck, and the sun deity Amaterasu, a few others include Fujin, the wind god; Susanoo, who brings storms; Ame-no-Uzume, the goddess of the dawn and dancing; and Tenjin, god of learning.

Ame-no-Uzume
Japan's goddess of the dawn and dancing

Once Buddhism arrived in Japan in the six century CE, near-mythic beings associated with it also expanded the Japanese

Fudo, the Immovable One

Of the so-called Guardians making up the Myo-o, a group of five Buddhist deities recognized in Japan, the best-known and arguably most powerful is Fudo Myo-o. His name means "immovable," a reference to his steadfast allegiance to upholding Buddhist religious concepts and laws. In mythology, Fudo supposedly opposes the forces of evil and does his best to eradicate them whenever possible. This is why Japanese artists typically depict him carrying a rope and a sword. The sword is meant to subdue the evil ones, and the rope is intended to bind them once they have been defeated. Artists also frequently show Fudo accompanied by two young assistants. One, named Kongara-doji, carries a lotus flower and stem, which signify the existing religious laws. The other helper, Seitaka-doji, holds a large gourd, which stands for the vastness of the universe. Although upholding religious laws is seen as Fudo's main godly duty, he is also the deity of mountain waterfalls.

mythos. Technically speaking, Buddhism has no supernatural divinities, nor one all-powerful deity like the God worshipped by Jews, Christians, and Muslims. Rather, Buddhism, which began in ancient India, is a philosophy of life that reveres the teachings of a man named Siddhartha, who, by discovering the causes of human suffering and how to alleviate it, became known as the Buddha, or "Enlightened One." Thereafter, in each new generation a few special individuals attained enlightenment and were seen as mentally and morally superior, but not divine. Some came to be called bodhisattvas.

When Buddhism spread to other Asian lands, however, peoples who had long worshipped groups of gods came to equate the leading bodhisattvas with some of their traditional deities. In Japan, for instance, people came to worship various bodhisattvas the same way they did the Shinto gods. The Japanese thereby developed a Buddhist pantheon of gods that coexists with the sacred Shinto pantheon. Among these Buddhist deities are the original Buddha, whom the Japanese call Shaka Nyorai; the powerful healer Yakushi Nyorai; Jizo Bosatsu, protector of children; and the Myo-o, or "Guardians," five deities thought to possess much wisdom and moral authority.

Boundless Kindness and Compassion

As was the case with the Shinto gods, background stories and other myths developed around most of the Japanese Buddhist deities. A well-known example consists of the tales about Kannon, Japan's bodhisattva of compassion and mercy. She is also known as a peacekeeper, a major proponent of vegetarianism, and the being to whom women who desire to become pregnant pray. Most commonly she is depicted holding a large, shiny jewel; it is believed that when she speaks while holding it, her words help bring a measure of success to human endeavors everywhere.

One of Kannon's more popular myths is her simple but elegant origin story. Of the many variations of it, the best-known version

Kannon emerged from a human tear and was known for her compassion.

claims she emerged from a human tear. That droplet was shed by Amitabha, a man who is believed to have attained enlightenment and then created a mystical kingdom where the spirits of morally good people could live after their deaths. To honor him, Kannon vowed to alleviate as much suffering as she could and help people become both ethical and enlightened.

To that end, the story goes, when Kannon entered Japan, she demonstrated her boundless compassion in several ways. One was to grant children to women who could not conceive. She also forgave and comforted people who had made mistakes and regretted them. Although Kannon helped thousands of people, at one point she expressed enormous regret that she could not aid still more. Hearing this, her mentor, Amitabha, reached out from his heavenly realm and gave her eleven heads and a thousand arms so that she could help many more struggling people.

This myth of Kannon's universal kindness and empathy explains why she is "one of the most beloved figures of Japanese mythology and belief," Ashkenazi writes. He adds that "she is the representative of pure mercy, and the major female figure in the mythology."[12]

The Dancing Deity

Another Japanese goddess, this one Shinto in origin, who was known for serving humanity was Ame-no-Uzume. Deity of the dawn, she was also the goddess of humor, dancing, and celebrations. In Japanese mythology she is credited with inventing not only formal dancing but also the other performing arts.

As Ame-no-Uzume's best-known tale begins, she was concerned to hear the news that the sun goddess, Amaterasu, had had a serious quarrel with her brother, the powerful kami Susanoo. During the altercation, Susanoo had become so upset that he had slaughtered one of Amaterasu's horses and splashed its blood on her sacred loom. Horrified, as well as insulted, the sun's overseer banished Susanoo and in a fit of anger retired to the depths of a large cave. Without her life-giving light, the world

From Greece to Japan?

Much has been made over the years about the strong religious and cultural influences of Buddhism and other East Asian religions on Japanese beliefs and mythology. Much less attention has been paid to mythological influences from areas beyond Asia. Of these, perhaps the clearest example is that of the Japanese wind god, the green-skinned Fujin. In the twentieth century, scholars traced his origins farther and farther westward along the Silk Route, the ancient network of trade routes that ran from East Asia, westward through the Middle East, to Europe. The present theory about Fujin centers on the invasion of western Asia by Greece's Alexander the Great in the 300s BCE. After his passing, some of his followers founded small kingdoms in the region and introduced Greek culture, including religious beliefs and gods. Over the centuries, apparently, the Greek wind god Boreas morphed into the Greco-Buddhist wind deity Wardo, who, over still more time, had Chinese and other East Asian counterparts. Eventually, the god in question reached Japan as Fujin. Tellingly, exactly like the much older Greek Boreas, Fujin's chief symbol is a leather bag filled with northerly, southerly, easterly, and westerly winds.

was plunged into darkness. And despite the pleas of hundreds of kami, she repeatedly refused to come out.

Ame-no-Uzume saw that most of the kami, along with virtually all the humans, were frightened. Without sunlight, plants withered and died, and it appeared that a terrible famine would soon arise. Hoping to avert such a disaster, Ame-no-Uzume conceived a bold plan designed to lure Amaterasu out of the cave. Near its entrance she hastily erected a wooden platform and asked the other gods to gather around it. As told by Indian historian Dattatreya Mandal, "she then started making cheery cries and it was followed up by gleeful dancing atop [the] platform. She even resorted to removing her clothes, which led to amusement among the other gods who started roaring in joy and laughter."[13]

Meanwhile, inside the cave Amaterasu could hear the commotion outside and decided to see what was causing it. Shoving aside the huge, heavy rock she had used to block the cave's entrance, she caught sight of Ame-no-Uzume doing her silly dance.

Dumbfounded by what appeared to be an embarrassing display, the sun deity walked outside, determined to reprimand her fellow goddess.

As Amaterasu approached the platform, several of the kami then present saw that she was distracted. Taking advantage of that fact, they hurried to the cave, pushed the rock back into place, and secured it with a magic rope that Amaterasu lacked the power to undo. In this way the sun goddess reentered the world, bringing back her life-giving light and warmth. She was one of the first to praise Ame-no-Uzume for her clever, daring plan, which had saved countless human lives.

An Extremely Versatile Deity

Still another deity that, according to legend, has helped enormous numbers of people over the centuries is Inari. Extremely versatile, this Shinto deity is sometimes depicted as male and other times female and is thought to embody traits of both genders. As a goddess she oversees the growing of tea and rice and in general strives to bring humanity prosperity. As a god, by contrast, Inari is thought to aid and protect human industries. One of those was metalworking and sword making. Therefore, Inari became particularly popular among the Samurai, a class of sword-wielding warriors who were prevalent in Japan from the 1500s to 1800s.

Inari

The Japanese deity of tea and rice growing, who also helps to bring prosperity to humanity

Inari is also strongly associated with *kitsune*, Japanese for "foxes," who supposedly carry messages for the deity. How Inari became associated with those unique animals is the subject of a popular tale. As Ashkenazi tells it:

> A pair of old magical foxes lived in the mountains. They were both of unusual appearance. The husband had silvery points on his fur, and the wife had the body of a fox but the head of a deer. They had five [offspring], equally

strange. One day they went and knelt before the shrine of Inari. They said, "Though we are dumb brutes, we are not without finer feelings, nor without sense, and we desire to serve the shrine in some capacity to do good." As a consequence, they and their brood were made the guardian assistants of Inari, as they remain, appearing in people's dreams and reporting what was going on to the kami.[14]

A man sees an apparition of Inari, who helps to bring human prosperity and often sends messages through foxes.

The foxes' desire to do good and help Inari spread prosperity is a perfect illustration of the way modern Japanese view their gods. Many of those deities are not just old, fanciful cultural references from the dim past, as are the Greek, Roman, and Norse gods. Rather, in modern Japan they are widely thought to be relevant. Inari, for instance, remains important to many members of the business classes. "Corporations still seek Inari's blessings when they break new ground," Gregory Wright points out, "and Inari is associated with not just corporate success but general prosperity for individuals, communities, and the country as a whole."[15]

A Host of Culture Heroes

Amakuni, a seventh-century Japanese blacksmith, saw himself as a humble sword maker and had no idea that future generations would call him a hero for the ages. When his emperor, Mommu, went to war, the soldiers in the army—the original Samurai warriors—naturally needed the sturdiest swords available. And Amakuni was among several blacksmiths called on to supply those weapons.

One day, following a particularly bloody battle, Amakuni and his son, Amakura, stood outside their workshop and watched a line of soldiers trudging back from the field of combat. Both father and son were struck by something disturbing: at least half of the fighters who passed by were carrying broken swords. In a moment of shocking awareness, says historian Angus Sutherland, Amakuni "realized that his weapons were useless. His disappointment overwhelmed him so much that he collected the remains of the swords to learn the reasons for their destruction. Was their design flawed? It took time for him to figure it out. He did not eat and drink water for seven days and nights, studying a better way to make swords."[16]

Mommu

The Japanese emperor who commissioned the blacksmith Amakuni to make new, improved swords for his soldiers

As this now famous tale continues, after much thought and hard work, the legendary sword maker conceived a momentous solution to the problem. First, he used a harder grade of steel on the weapon's outer edge. Second, and particularly crucial, he made that edge curved instead of straight. As a result, the sword was far more resistant to shocks and much less likely to break than earlier straight versions.

Employing the revolutionary new design, the two smiths worked tirelessly during the winter months making new swords for Mommu's army. And when spring came and the emperor launched a new military campaign, all the warriors were equipped with the new weapons. More than two weeks passed, and word came that there had been another major battle. Once again Amakuni and Amakura stood outside their workshop to watch the returning soldiers. This time, thankfully, not a single broken sword could be seen.

A Samurai holds his sword in battle. The Samurai sword was invented by Amakuni, a seventh-century Japanese blacksmith.

And then a man dressed in a striking suit of blood-spattered armor climbed down from his horse and approached the two smiths. "Who might this be?" Amakura whispered to his father. Amakuni smiled broadly because he knew the man was the emperor himself. Mommu returned the smile and in a gesture that amazed all who saw it, bowed to the father and son. "You are an expert sword maker," the emperor said (according to Sutherland). "None of the swords you made failed in this battle."[17] Thereafter, Amakuni's invention, the renowned Samurai sword, became the weapon of choice for Japanese warriors.

Invention, Loyalty, and Honor

It is not uncommon for people who are learning about the Japanese myths for the first time to be surprised that Amakuni's story is listed alongside those of famous warriors and monster slayers. But the truth is that many of the Japanese mythical heroes do not fit the familiar pattern that the heroes of many other world mythologies follow. Indeed, not all the Japanese ones are valiant fighters who slay marauding beasts and tyrants or combat injustice. Some Japanese heroes do fit that profile, including a fair number of skilled Samurai fighters, yet their motives are not always unselfish, and they sometimes hurt as many people as they help. As Michael Ashkenazi points out, several of them "are not by the standards of the modern world necessarily wholly admirable. Many are avaricious [greedy], and some vicious and destructive. . . . The character of most of the [warrior] heroes of Japanese myth is, at least, ambiguous. They are prepared to use all means, fair and foul, to attain their goal. Most of them are graced by physical prowess, and many of them come to tragic ends."[18]

Other Japanese mythical characters qualify as heroic because they advanced Japanese culture in one way or another, often by inventing or discovering something important. Amakuni has long been a frequently cited example. Another is Nomi no Sukune, who founded sumo wrestling, a highly respected athletic and social institution in Japan.

Fulfilling the Definition of a Classic Hero

The renowned modern mythologist Joseph Campbell once defined the type of classic hero who appears in all world mythologies, saying that "a hero ventures forth from the world of common day into a region of supernatural wonder. Fabulous forces are there encountered and a decisive victory is won. The hero comes back from this mysterious adventure with the power to bestow boons on his fellow man."

Campbell's definition of a classic mythical hero fits many of the heroic characters in surviving Japanese folklore, according to scholars at England's famous Toshidama Gallery, which restores and displays ancient Japanese art. As an example, the Toshidama experts cite the legendary Japanese hero Minamoto Raike. In his most famous story, he hears that an oni, or huge demon, has turned a nearby region into a haunted countryside. Rushing to the scene, Raike disguises himself as a religious scholar and talks the demon into drinking a magic liquor that causes extreme drowsiness. Thereby, the creature falls asleep and Raike kills it. Fulfilling Campbell's definition of a hero, the boon that Raike bestows on humanity is to make the haunted countryside safe for people to settle in.

Joseph Campbell, *The Hero with a Thousand Faces.* Princeton, NJ: Princeton University Press, 1949, p. 30.

Still other so-called heroes are recognized for acts of kindness or participating in unusual adventures. In one myth, for instance, a young fisherman, Urashima, saves the life of a small sea turtle from cruel children. The turtle bears Urashima on its back and leads him to an underwater palace. The creature turns out to be a sea god's daughter in disguise. Urashima enjoys a few days in the palace and is gifted with a box that will keep him safe if he never opens it. Reluctantly bidding goodbye, he returns to the surface, where he is shocked to discover that hundreds of years have passed. Disconsolate, he opens the box. He sees it is empty, but a smoke arises from it that ages Urashima rapidly into an old man, for it contained the years he avoided while residing in the magical underwater realm. The tale teaches people the value of kindness but reminds them that time waits for no one. Even today, nearly all Japanese children learn Urashima's story at an early age, and he remains one of Japan's principal folk heroes.

Because characters like Urashima inhabit tales that mix the virtues of doing good with the woes or harsh truths that come from everyday living, the Japanese tend to see them as culture heroes. Whatever their protagonist's motives, goals, and deeds may be, many stories emphasize one or both of two primary themes in Japanese myth. One is a struggle against extensive, sometimes even hopeless, odds. And the result is sometimes defeat, but defeat with honor. The other major theme of Japan's heroic myths is loyalty, whether to one's family, boss, or military leader. These highlight prevailing Japanese cultural ethics—the virtue of personal honor even at the expense of one's life. That almost sacred principle dictates—even today—that every individual should avoid being dishonorable at all costs.

The Amazing Peach Boy

The importance of both loyalty and honor is stressed in one of Japan's classic hero myths—the tale of the Momotaro, commonly nicknamed the Peach Boy. The reason for that rather charming appellation was that he supposedly emerged from a giant peach. An elderly, childless woman discovered this peach in the river in which she was washing clothes. Taking the fruit home, she showed it to her husband, and they began slicing it open to eat it.

Momotaro
The so-called Peach Boy, said to have been born from inside a giant peach

To the couple's surprise, however, out of the peach popped a small but muscular male child dressed in full battle armor. "Don't be afraid," the boy said, as told by the noted early modern Japanese translator and storyteller Yei Theodora Ozaki. "I am no demon or fairy. I will tell you the truth. Heaven has had compassion on you. Every day and every night you have lamented that you had no child. Your cry has been heard and I am sent to be the son of your old age."[19]

Delighted, the couple named the youngster Momotaro (from the words *momo*, meaning "peach," and *taro*, or "eldest son"). The three lived in harmony for a few years. During that period the boy demonstrated amazing strength, military skills, and courage, attributes he claimed came from the gods.

When Momotaro was fifteen, he told his parents that he reluctantly had to leave them for a while to fight a band of *oni*—ogres, demons, and other nasty creatures—infesting an island off Japan's coast. They were thieves, murderers, and cannibals, he explained, and were victimizing the island's human inhabitants. "These devils are very hateful beings," he added. "I must go and conquer them."[20]

Bidding his parents farewell, the young warrior crossed overland toward the island. On the way he interacted and became friends with a monkey, a dog, and a pheasant, all of whom could speak fluent Japanese. The three agreed to aid Momotaro in his noble quest. And they were true to their word. Reaching the island, the four comrades slew hundreds of oni, after which they captured both the creatures' stronghold and the chief ogre. In Ozaki's words, "The whole country made a hero of Momotaro on his triumphant return, and rejoiced that [Japan] was now freed from the robber devils who had been a terror of the land for a long time."[21]

An elderly, childless woman found a peach in the river when she was washing clothes, and she discovered Momotaro inside it.

A Mythical Hero Becomes a Media Hero

One of Japan's most memorable mythical heroes, Kintaro, the so-called Golden Boy, has become one of the best-known characters in modern Japanese literature, art, and entertainment media. For instance, each year numerous plays about him are staged in Japanese grade schools and middle schools. Based in part on his happy times with his animal pals, those productions typically promote the importance of treating animals with respect and kindness. Meanwhile, Japanese films, TV shows, and video games depict Kintaro going on quests to fight scary monsters and evil humans. The Golden Boy is also celebrated in various public festivals and artistic displays. Each year, for example, several Japanese cities hold parades that feature floats depicting his adventures. Also, it has become customary in various parts of the country for people to set up shrines decorated with paintings and sculptures of him, especially ones that show him cavorting with this animal friends. In these and other ways, Japanese musician and artist Yudai Kato says, "Kintaro remains an enduring symbol in Japanese mythology, representing the power of youth, the importance of courage, and the beauty of the natural world."

Yudai Kato, "Kintaro: The Golden Boy of the Mountains," Japanese Mythology, November 11, 2024. https://japanese.mythologyworldwide.com.

The Golden Boy

Another legendary Japanese hero who showed unusual strength and courage when young was Kintaro, which means "Golden Boy." His parents, who were deeply in love, hailed from the city of Kyoto. When the father died unexpectedly, the grieving mother moved to a small cabin in a distant forest and soon afterward gave birth to Kintaro.

Almost immediately she noticed that he possessed amazing strength for an infant, and over time he grew even stronger. At age eight, the boy was able to cut down and haul away a large tree in an hour, a job that normally took three grown woodcutters a full day. Not surprisingly, the local woodsmen who witnessed his feats called him "Wonder Child." Yet despite his seemingly superhuman physical prowess, he was often remarkably gentle. That came in handy when he played with his best friends—a rabbit, a deer, a monkey, and a bear. He frequently wrestled with them in a meadow near his home and was always careful not to injure them.

One day the five friends came to a stream they wanted to cross. And when they saw that the water was too turbulent to do so safely, Kintaro said not to worry because he would build a bridge. As Ozaki told it, the boy walked to "a very large tree that was growing at the water's edge. He took hold of the trunk and pulled it with all his might, once, twice, thrice! At the third pull, so great was Kintaro's strength that the roots gave way, and . . . over fell the tree, forming an excellent bridge across the stream."[22]

What Kintaro did not realize at the time was that a Japanese military general who was walking through the forest on his way to Kyoto had witnessed the creation of the bridge. Astounded at what he had seen, the man visited the boy's mother and convinced her to let him take Kintaro to the city. There, the general said, the child would be allowed to engage in military training and make a name for himself.

Not only did the mother agree, but the child was also thrilled at the prospect of becoming a soldier. He happily accompanied the general to Kyoto, and there the boy began his training. The speed at which he advanced through the military ranks proved phenomenal. Moreover, when a giant monster appeared and ravaged the countryside near Kyoto, Kintaro, then in his teens, singlehandedly attacked and beheaded it. It is no wonder, therefore, that in the centuries that followed, the Golden Boy took a well-earned place on the list of the greatest heroes in Japan's history.

Oto's Brave Sacrifice

Although a great many of Japan's culture heroes—including Kintaro, Momotaro, and Amakuni—were men, there were some female ones as well. Among those memorable women was the courageous Oto Tachibana. As a child, she was unaware that she had been born on the very same day as her future husband and fellow hero, Prince Ousu, also known as Yamato Takeru.

Oto Tachibana

A courageous woman who sacrificed her life to save her husband from almost certain death

As a teenager, Oto became enamored of the sun goddess, Amaterasu. Desiring to become a guardian of one of that deity's major shrines, the girl studied martial arts and became a skilled warrior. Eventually, after being accepted as one of the shrine's protectors, Oto helped guard an artifact sacred to the goddess, the White Bird Mirror.

The young woman was naturally upset when a band of thieves managed to sneak into the shrine and steal the mirror. Hoping to retrieve the object, Oto gathered her weapons and some sup-

Oto Tachibana was born on the same day as her future husband—Yamato Takeru—for whom she later sacrificed her life.

plies and began tracking down the thieves. The journey took her to the Japanese kingdom of Yamato. And there, by chance, she met Yamato Takeru. The two instantly fell deeply in love and soon married, after which she accompanied him on an official mission assigned to him by his father, Emperor Keiko.

Reaching the edge of what is now Tokyo Bay, Yamato hired some boats to take him, Oto, and their followers across. But as Joshua Frydman relates:

> In the middle of their crossing the sky grew dark and a sudden storm raged over the sea. Yamato Takeru's men were frightened, but Oto Tachibana spoke up suddenly. She claimed that the storm was the doing of Watasumi, the god of the sea, and that if he could take her instead, he would let Yamato Takeru pass. Yamato Takeru and all his men wept, but they took the brave Oto Tachibana and released her into the ocean. She sank down into the water and immediately the storm cleared.[23]

In sacrificing her life for someone she dearly loved, Oto demonstrated the loyalty that is so prized in Japanese myth and society. Over time, her tale would be told often in film, on television, and in video games. These media, along with written and oral tales, would ceaselessly celebrate her selfless deed as they have done for many other heroes of Japanese culture.

Animals, Creatures, and Monsters

A medieval Japanese farmer named Akinosuke was planting crops when he saw some friends approaching with food and drink. Taking a break from his work, he enjoyed a meal with his guests and then fell asleep under an old cedar tree. On awakening, he was surprised to see that his friends had departed without saying goodbye.

Akinosuke

A farmer who dreams in his sleep that he falls in love with and has children with a woman—only to learn later that the woman is really an ant

At that moment Akinosuke noticed a long line of well-dressed people walking toward him. He soon learned that they were members of the royal court of the king of Tokoga. That name seemed familiar to Akinosuke. In fact, he could have sworn that it was an imaginary realm spoken of only in stories told to children at bedtime. Apparently, however, it must be real, he said to himself, since the courtiers claimed to hail from there.

Those visitors led the perplexed farmer to their king's palace, where that ruler welcomed Akinosuke and treated him to a lavish feast. At the conclusion of the meal, the king announced that Akinosuke was scheduled to marry the kingdom's beautiful princess the next day. Astounded and completely confused, Akinosuke felt himself swept along in a flurry of unexpected events. The marriage did indeed take place, and a few days later he and his new bride traveled to a nearby island and moved into a splendid mansion. There, they lived happily for seven years, during which the princess bore Akinosuke several healthy children.

As the marriage's eighth year began, however, the still young and vital woman died suddenly of unknown causes. By this time Akinosuke was deeply in love with her, and he was therefore heartbroken at her passing. He held a magnificent funeral for her in which the mourners placed her highly decorated coffin beneath a large, oval-shaped stone.

No sooner had the ceremony ended than a messenger from the king told Akinosuke that he needed to return to the capital. Boarding a royal barge, he reluctantly left the island. Halfway into the journey he turned to gaze lovingly on the place in which he had dwelled so contentedly for so long. But to his abject horror, the island was no longer there.

With an audible gasp, Akinosuke awakened to find himself back under the ancient cedar tree. A half-eaten apple was in his hand, and his friends were just finishing lunch. They told him that he had been napping for only a few minutes but that something odd had occurred. While he was sleeping, a butterfly had flown out of his mouth. It landed on the ground, where some ants dragged it under the tree. Moreover, a second before Akinosuke awakened, the butterfly had reappeared and flown back into his mouth.

Someone suggested that the butterfly was Akinosuke's soul, which prompted the men to examine the ground near the tree. There they found a large colony of ants and a few feet away a smaller colony. In the center of that smaller colony, Akinosuke noticed a small, oval-shaped stone. And when he lifted it, he saw a tiny, decorated coffin in which rested the body of a female ant.

A Fascination for Nature's Fauna

One of the most beloved and often retold Japanese myths, "The Dream of Akinosuke" is one of many that deal with the connection between humans and animals. In this case the animals involved are insects. But Japanese mythology is filled with stories about animals of almost all kinds, many of which have mystical powers and can talk.

This fascination for mythical, fanciful depictions of nature's fauna was well illustrated in ancient Japan by an intense interest in the so-called four sky gods. All four are animals seemingly possessing magical qualities. The equivalent of modern sky constellations, they are Genbu, the black warrior of the north; Byakko, the white tiger of the west; Suzaku, the red bird of the south; and Seiryu, the blue dragon of the east. Images of these creatures have long appeared in Japanese cultural events, religious celebrations, and literature.

Also, each appeared in at least one myth. For instance, Byakko was born an ordinary tiger, but one that lived a very long time. When it reached the age of five hundred, it turned white and ac-

This picture shows a demon cat and a fox spirit. Japanese mythology contains many animals who can talk like people.

quired mystical powers, including the ability to control the wind. It has come to symbolize the west and the windy autumn season.

Among the other animals that have fantastic forms or abilities and interact with people in the Japanese myths, foxes are frequent and popular. Shape-shifters, they often change into beautiful women or elderly people. And some of them try to swindle humans. But not all the mythical foxes are mischievous or mean-spirited. For instance, the foxes that act as the goddess Inari's messengers are a well-known exception.

The Sociable Snake-Man

Dragons, snakes, and other reptiles are also popular in the Japanese myths. Often, they appear as evil or sinister in European and other Western myths. However, in Japanese tales they tend to be friendly, benevolent, and sources of wisdom.

One of the more famous of these Japanese mythical reptiles is the *uwabami*, or giant snake. Most of its kind have magical powers, including shape-shifting, and although some are primitive, scary, and eat people whole, others are intelligent, sociable, and ethical. In one popular myth, for instance, a well-educated, kindhearted uwabami often enjoyed morphing into a handsome young man. And one day he and an attractive young human woman met and fell in love.

Wanting to politely follow social custom, the snake-man went to the girl's father, a wealthy landowner, and asked for her hand in marriage. But the father, who was repulsed by snakes, said no and secretly set a deadly trap that almost killed the uwabami. In retaliation, according to Japan-based folklorist Matthew Meyer, the determined suitor used his powers to conjure up a massive storm. "Rain the likes of which had never been seen before fell," Meyers writes. "[A local lake] swelled in size and burst forth, flooding everything around. All of the villages surrounding the lake were annihilated. Houses were knocked down. Fields were flooded and washed away."[24]

Giant Monsters That Attack Cities

One of the best-known categories of Japanese mythical creatures goes by the name *kaiju*. Among the ancient Japanese, this was a general term for any legendary, scary creature, much like the general English term *monster*. But today kaiju are now characterized as giant monsters that attack cities. The first major depiction of modern kaiju was the 1954 movie *Godzilla*. In the story, that huge beast is awakened by nuclear testing in the Pacific Ocean. And historians say that that creature, and other modern kaiju, initially symbolized the destructive power of the atomic bombs dropped on the Japanese cities of Hiroshima and Nagasaki in World War II. Indeed, says scholar Joshua Frydman, Ishiro Honda, the director of the 1954 film, wanted to make an allegory about the suffering the war had caused, so he depicted the monster as "a force of nature, unstoppable and indestructible." In this way, "the Japanese film industry gave birth to a new myth that represents both the fears and hopes of modern society." And that film has led to many in a series of kaiju movies, perpetuating new myths that reflect Japan's strengths and fears.

Joshua Frydman, *The Japanese Myths: A Guide to Gods, Heroes, and Spirits*. London: Thames and Hudson, 2022, p. 208.

Unfortunately for all concerned, the young woman the snake-man loved died in the flood. Grief-stricken, he quickly caused the raging waters to subside. And for the rest of his life, for fear of hurting anyone else, he refrained from using his powers.

A Scary Ogre Meets Its Match

Japanese mythology is also filled with strange creatures and monsters that are neither human nor animal and whose looks and actions tend to be unpleasant or scary. The members of the biggest single group of these beings are called *yokai*. According to Joshua Frydman, they can be roughly defined as "spirits of the countryside." Often, he says, they "take monstrous or bizarre forms. Many modern works translate the term *yokai* as 'demon,' 'devil,' or 'monster' in English. This is an easy shorthand for explaining [them], but . . . they are not necessarily evil any more than any wild animal or natural phenomenon. Some prefer to do evil, but . . . some are also sources of great good."[25]

oni
Giants, or ogres, who live in remote, mountainous areas and sometimes raid human villages

Of the many types of yokai in Japanese myths, probably the best known are the oni. They most often take the form of large ogres or hideous trolls. Oni supposedly inhabited ancient Japan's mountainous regions and sometimes raided nearby human villages to steal food or kidnap children.

One of the best-known stories featuring an oni is the myth of Issun Boshi, the "Inch-High Warrior." As the tale commences, an aging childless couple desperately desired to have a youngster of their own. To that end, they prayed to a god, and sure enough, the deity answered their plea by granting them a baby boy. Although they loved the child dearly, there was a problem: he never grew any taller than an inch. Thus, they named him Issun Boshi, or "One-Inch Boy."

When Issun reached young adulthood, he decided to go out and try to exert some sort of positive impact on the world. For a while he traveled in a boat fashioned from a rice bowl, used a chopstick for a paddle, and carried a sword made from a sewing needle. Soon he came to the mansion of the governor of his province. When Issun sought an

The best known of the many types of yokai in Japanese myths are the oni. They most often take the form of large ogres or hideous trolls. Oni supposedly inhabited ancient Japan's mountainous regions and sometimes raided nearby villages.

audience with that official, however, the governor's assistants simply laughed at him on account of his minuscule size.

The next day, while Issun was sitting, forlorn, near the mansion, a huge, terrifying oni appeared and broke into the structure. Seconds later, the giant exited, carrying the governor's daughter in one hand. As the beast trudged off, Issun followed it, running as fast as his little legs allowed.

The tiny pursuer finally caught up to the oni in a clearing in a nearby forest. In a loud voice, he ordered the oni to release the girl. But the towering monster simply chuckled, grabbed Issun, and swallowed him. Down the giant's gullet the one-inch warrior tumbled, until he found himself in the oni's belly. Wasting no time, the fearless little fighter began jabbing his needle sword into the walls of the creature's enormous gut. As blood squirted in all directions, the oni bellowed in pain, dropped the girl onto the ground, and vomited up his teensy attacker.

Immediately, Issun urged the girl to run. But it turned out to be unnecessary, for it was the wounded, terrified ogre that ran

Lifeless Objects That Become Conscious

Of all the Japanese mythical creatures, perhaps the strangest are called *tsukumogami*. These lifeless objects—such as teakettles, lanterns, dinner plates, shoes, and so forth—can suddenly spring to life of their own accord. However, according to the lore, such an object must be part of a human household for a minimum of one hundred years. Once that is achieved, the object acquires a sort of soul, becomes conscious, and can move from place to place. What happens next often depends on what kind of relationship the object and owner had in the past, says Italian scholar Mauro Piacentini. The myths about tsukumogami, he explains, suggest "that objects that have absorbed anger, rancor, [or] contempt can then turn into dangerous things for those who own them. But at the same time objects that have 'grown' with affection, with a benevolent feeling towards them and others, can become 'good' objects some of which even sacrifice themselves for [their owners]." Tsukumogami were once used to impart Buddhist teachings, but in the modern era, they often reflect humanity's careless regard or neglect for everyday things.

Mauro Piacentini, "Tsukumogami: When Objects Take Life," Fukai Nihon, 2025. www.fukainihon.org.

kappa
Human-shaped creatures having green, scaly skin and beaks like those of turtles

and did not stop till it reached the mountain cave it called home. As for Issun, he said yes when the grateful governor insisted that he marry his daughter. And thereafter, no one ever laughed at Issun Boshi again.

An Imaginative Array of Creatures

Many other kinds of yokai appear in the Japanese myths, along with other similar creatures and monsters. A prominent example consists of the *bake-danuki*, or "monster racoons." Bigger than ordinary racoons and able to shape-shift into human form, they are said to enjoy playing pranks on humans and occasionally robbing them. More dangerous and fearsome are the *kappa*. Although humanoid in shape, they have green, scaly skin and beaks like those of turtles. In the myths, kappa dwell in lakes and rivers and when possible seize people and devour their livers. No less strange and frightening are the *yamanba*, aged witches who have a strong craving for human flesh.

In a few cases, even creepy-looking mythical creatures are not overtly dangerous to humans and can even be beneficial in some way. Perhaps the best-known example is the *ningyo*, which is half fish and half human. What makes this creature especially unusual in the old tales is that a

The ningyo is half human and half fish. Anyone who eats its flesh becomes immortal.

person who eats its flesh supposedly becomes immortal and can die only by murder or suicide.

One of the best-known myths about ningyo begins when a fisherman unexpectedly caught one that had just died. The man cooked the creature but did not eat any of it because he had no desire to live forever. But he did give some of the meat to his extremely ill daughter, hoping it would save her life. Frydman recalls the results, saying that she got well "and grew up healthy and beautiful. However, once she reached adulthood, the girl stopped ageing. She eventually took Buddhist vows after her husband and children died, and lived for 800 years, wandering Japan as a deathless nun. Eventually she returned to her home village and ended her own life."[26]

Whether the animals, creatures, and monsters of the Japanese myths are beneficial, mischievous, or lethal, they have two things in common. First, they are numerous, occupying every conceivable niche in nature. Second, they take an incredible array of imaginative, creative forms. Says University of California scholar Michael D. Foster:

> The primary driving factor behind [the Japanese mythical creatures] then and now is simply the power of human creativity. Despite the fact that they have been around for centuries, [they] always reflect a spirit of imagination, inventiveness, change and, ultimately, possibility. I have suggested that [they] are born from the human need to explain the unexplainable, and in this context they are nothing more than highly creative metaphors for things for which we have no words.[27]

Feats of the Divine Hachiman

Late one summer afternoon in eleventh-century Japan, the powerful Samurai lord Minamoto Yoriyoshi received some disturbing news. Leader of the renowned Minamoto clan and commander of the Japanese emperor's northern armies, Yoriyoshi had sent a spy to Hokkaido two weeks previously to learn about a troubling conflict there. Hokkaido is the northernmost of the country's larger islands and had long been a disputed territory. A local people known as the Ainu claimed that island belonged to them because they had been its first inhabitants. Yoriyoshi's spy now confirmed that bands of Ainu were harassing Japanese farmers who had recently settled there.

Minamoto Yoshiie

A Japanese military general who supposedly received valuable advice from Hachiman

Realizing it was his duty to move against the Ainu, Yoriyoshi summoned his grown son, Minamoto Yoshiie. The younger man was widely seen as one of the two or three most skilled Samurai warriors in all of Japan and a gifted military general. On three occasions he had led the Minamoto forces to victory in battles with rebels who had defied the emperor. These successes had earned Yoshiie the nickname of Hachiman Taro, "Son of Hachiman." This was an honorable title to be sure, because Hachiman, god of war, was one of the most beloved and respected Japanese deities.

When Yoshiie arrived at his father's mansion, the elder Minamoto assigned him the task of going to Hokkaido and putting the troublesome Ainu in their place. Eagerly, the son gathered more than a thousand warriors and hurried to southern Hokkaido. He was certain that he would achieve a swift victory over the enemy. That attitude soon proved to be overconfident, however, for the Ainu fighters wisely avoided a pitched battle against a superior force. They chose instead to divert most of the streams in the area, thereby severely reducing the fresh water available to the Samurai.

When the Minamoto troops finally ran out of water, the desperate Yoshiie went to his tent and prayed to his namesake, Hachiman, for aid. The prevailing belief was that the war god favored the Minamoto clan and had bestowed upon Yoshiie the military skills that had made his earlier victories possible. Sure enough, mere minutes after the young man had uttered the prayer, it was answered. An almost blinding light filled the tent, and a tall figure stepped out of that radiant glow. Dropping to his knees, Yoshiie beheld a towering warrior clad in gleaming armor, with eyes that emitted a fiery orange-red glow. The awestruck man begged the god to help him in his moment of need.

Minamoto Yoshiie was one of the most skilled Samurai in Japan. He earned the nickname "Son of Hachiman."

Hachiman and the Rebel Warlord

One of the several surviving myths about the war god Hachiman involves his supposed role in a real military rebellion against Japan's imperial government in the 900s CE. The trouble began when Taira Masakado, a warlord based in eastern Japan, attacked and defeated some fellow warlords. Then, according to a story he propagated, which thereafter became part of Japan's collected myths, he spoke directly to the divine Hachiman. Purportedly, Masakado went to one of the god's shrines, and there Hachiman appeared to him and told him that he—Masakado—was the rightful emperor. The god said that his attacks on other warlords were justified and that he should not stop until he had taken over the government and sat on the throne. As might be expected, the reigning emperor, Suzaku, had no intention of stepping down. He declared Masakado an outlaw and sent an army to eliminate him. Fifty-nine days later, Masakado was defeated and beheaded. But for many centuries to come, people in several Japanese provinces believed the myth about Hachiman's endorsement of the rebellion and that Masakado did deserve to be emperor.

In response, Hachiman told Yoshiie to exit the tent and shoot an arrow into the nearest boulder. Obediently, the Samurai commander did so, and when the missile struck the rock, fresh water began to gush outward, forming a new stream. Thrilled, Yoshiie ran back to the tent, intent on thanking the god. But Hachiman was gone. As he had done in the past, and would do again in the future, he had protected Japan and its emperor against any outside forces that threatened them.

An Increasingly Beloved God

That image of Hachiman—as Japan's chief divine protector—remained steadfast for century after century. And in fact, even today many Japanese believe he still cares about and watches over them. Furthermore, those who believe in him accept most or all the mythical feats credited to him as real historical events. It is no wonder, as many modern historians have pointed out, that there are more shrines across Japan dedicated to him than to any other deity. By the early 2020s the number was more than thirty thousand.

Jingu
The Japanese empress who gave birth to Ojin, the emperor who later became Hachiman

In addition to Hachiman's role as Japan's protector, another reason he is so widely venerated is his strong connection to the country's imperial family. The sun goddess, Amaterasu, remains the main mythical ancestor of the long line of Japanese emperors, but Hachiman's link to those rulers is no less potent, because the myths say he began as one of them. An empress named Jingu, the story goes, gave birth to a son name Ojin, who eventually sat on the throne as the fifteenth emperor. According to legend, he possessed exceptional military skills, and during his reign Japan expanded in size and its people were safe and happy.

Because he had been such an extraordinary leader, over time—an estimated two to three centuries—he became increasingly beloved by the Japanese people. And according to legend, they repeatedly prayed that he be made into a god. According to one surviving myth, Amaterasu and several other deities listened and used their divine powers to transform Ojin into a kami when he died. Thus, the deceased Ojin became the war god Hachiman.

Hachiman's popularity grew when the Samurai warrior class adopted him as their patron god. According to Hirafuji Kikuko, a professor at Japan's Kokugakuin University:

> During the middle ages, the powerful Minamoto clan took Hachiman as their *ujigami* (clan deity), helping propagate the worship of the deity even further. . . . [The Minamoto leaders] inaugurated nearly 700 years of warrior rule in Japan, and subsequent military leaders sought the divine support of Hachiman, bolstering the popularity of the deity among the warrior class. . . . In time Hachiman became the mostly widely venerated kami in Japan.[28]

A Deep Concern for Children

While revered as a patron of warriors, Hachiman was also portrayed as a divine protector of Japan's children. That aspect of his character derived from one of the ancient tales involving the empress Jingu and her son.

The myth recounts a serious disagreement between Jingu and her husband (and Ojin's father), the emperor Chuai. A local warlord challenged Chuai's authority, and in response, the emperor began preparing his troops for battle.

The problem was that Jingu claimed to have been visited and for a short time possessed by the sea god Watatsumi, who had insisted that Japan must invade Korea instead of fighting a petty warlord. When the empress told Chuai about the visitation, he dismissed it as nonsense. Angered, Watatsumi slew the emperor in his sleep.

With her husband dead, Jingu, then pregnant with Ojin, took control of the imperial army and invaded Korea as the sea god had demanded. During the campaign, the story goes,

Jingu sets foot in Korea following the death of her husband. The sea god Watatsumi had told her that Japan must invade Korea.

the empress suddenly experienced intense labor pains. Not wanting the child to be born amid the dangers of war, she tied a rock to her waist in order to suppress the contractions and continued leading the army. She managed to keep the child within her and well protected for three years before returning to Japan and giving birth. As time went on, Ojin inherited her deep concern for protecting children, and that concern for young people's safety remained with him when he was transformed into Hachiman.

Lead-Up to a Miracle

It is inarguable that Hachiman's background as a former emperor, along with his roles as protector of children and mentor of the warrior class, made him highly respected across Japan. However, these and his other qualities and achievements were ultimately overshadowed by a feat of epic proportions. By far his greatest claim to fame and what made him beloved by all future generations of Japanese was the belief that he saved the country from utter destruction. Moreover, his myths claimed, he did so twice in the space of only a few years.

Kublai Khan
The Mongol leader who overran China but tried and twice failed to conquer Japan

The first of these miracles, as the Japanese viewed them, occurred in 1274 CE. In the lead-up to that pivotal year, Kublai Khan, a Mongol leader who at that time ruled much of China, was at war with those Chinese who remained independent of the Mongols. He wanted to eventually defeat the Southern Song, the leaders of those still-free Chinese. The Khan knew that Japan regularly traded with the Southern Song. And he wanted to convince the Japanese to cease that trade to economically weaken the Song rulers. To that end, the Khan sent an emissary to Japan to negotiate a deal.

What the Mongol ruler did not foresee, however, was that the Japanese emperor wanted nothing to do with the Mongols and their power struggles. He therefore refused even to talk to the

Emperor Ojin's Many Accomplishments

It is no wonder that the Japanese people ended up deifying the emperor Ojin and thereby creating the war god Hachiman, says historian Wu Mingren. After all, explains Wu,

> numerous important political and cultural contributions to Japanese society are attributed to Ojin. For instance, the emperor is credited with the consolidation of imperial power, and the institution of land reforms. Moreover, he is believed to have been an active promoter of cultural exchange with Korea and China. Thanks to these foreign interactions, Korean weaving techniques, the Chinese writing system, and [the Chinese philosophy] Confucianism were introduced in Japan. . . .
>
> Considering that Ojin made many significant contributions to Japanese society, it is not entirely surprising that he was deified after his death. This deification process, however, did not take place immediately after he died, but many centuries later . . . it is now commonly accepted that Hachiman and the deified Ojin are one and the same. . . .

Wu Mingren, "Hachiman: Deified Emperor, War God, Protector of the Japanese People," Ancient Origins, January 13, 2021. www.ancient-origins.net.

Khan's emissary. Annoyed at being ignored by a tiny country with an army far smaller than his own, Kublai Khan sent more emissaries, this time with demands, but they were ignored as well. Now very angry, the Khan decided to conquer Japan, and he spent months amassing an invasion force consisting of at least five hundred ships and thirty thousand men.

The First Divine Wind

In the autumn of 1274, the fleet launched and quickly made it to Hakata Bay, on the western coast of Japan's Kyushu Island. The Mongol commander wasted no time in sending a few thousand troops ashore, and there they fought a battle with a smaller force of Japanese warriors. The Samurai were disadvantaged not only in numbers but also in weaponry. According to Tama University historian Kawai Atsushi:

> The Mongol soldiers' short bows had greater range than those of the [Samurai] and their arrows were tipped with poison, making even glancing hits fatal to the Japanese. Horses as well as soldiers came under attack. Alongside the clamor of gongs, the [Mongols] deployed explosive projectiles. Gunpowder was still unknown in Japan; the black shells that exploded midair, releasing fire and smoke, amazed Japan's warriors and terrified its horses so that they could not fight. Under such conditions, the [Samurai] had no choice but to retreat.[29]

Despite having the upper hand, as the sun set the invaders returned to their ships, apparently to rest up before attacking in larger numbers the next day. "That night," however, historical writer Joanna Gillan relates, seemingly out of nowhere an enormous storm "struck as the ships lay at anchor in Hakata Bay. By daybreak, only a few ships remained. The rest were destroyed, taking the lives of thousands of Mongols with them."[30]

When the Mongols tried to attack Japan, their fleet was devastated by a storm, and the Samurai killed any survivors.

According to the myths associated with Hachiman, word of this incredible event spread swiftly throughout Japan. Untold thousands of people had been praying to Hachiman to save them, and he had promptly done so. Mere hours after the invaders had arrived, the story went, he had sent his kamikaze, or "divine wind," to annihilate the invaders. A common variant of the tale was that Hachiman had been aided in creating the typhoon by the storm god Raijin and wind god Fujin.

The Second Divine Wind

Although the Japanese were certain that divine forces had wrecked the enemy fleet, Kublai Khan saw it as merely a case of unfortunate timing. Due to coincidence and bad luck, he contended, his fleet had arrived in Japan just as a massive storm was about to strike. Still determined to subjugate Japan, seven years later, in 1281, he sent a far larger invasion force. According to Gillan, the fleet consisted of more than 4,000 ships and 70,000 to 140,000 troops. "One set of forces set out from Korea," she says, "while another set sail from southern China, converging near Hakata Bay in August, 1281."[31]

On August 15 the invaders were ready to launch a huge assault on western Kyushu. In the distance, they could see a few thousand Samurai guarding the beaches. But surely, the Mongol commander reasoned, these locals would be no match for the enormous forces he was about to unleash.

As it turned out, however, the Mongol general was never able to unleash those forces, because once again a tremendous typhoon struck the area. Gillan points out that "contemporary Japanese accounts indicate that over 4,000 ships were destroyed and 80 percent of the soldiers either drowned or were killed by Samurai on the beaches in what became one of the largest and most disastrous attempts at a naval invasion in history. The Mongols never attacked Japan again."[32]

No one knows how Kublai Khan interpreted the destruction of his second fleet and whether he once more attributed the losses to bad luck. But among the Japanese there was no question of what had happened. Their war god, perhaps aided by Fujin and Raijin, had once again made possible the survival of the Japanese people and their homeland.

Today, close to eight centuries later, many people in Japan remain beholden to Hachiman. The mythological website Avid Archer aptly sums up his legacy, saying that within Japanese culture he continues to exert "multifaceted influence." And worship of him at his numerous shrines "continues to resonate within the collective consciousness of Japan, thus underscoring his timeless relevance."[33]

Introduction: The Phantom's Secret

1. Quoted in Lizzie Vaughan, *Tales of Japan*. San Francisco: Chronicle Books, 2019, p. 105.
2. Quoted in Vaughan, *Tales of Japan*, p. 107.
3. Daniel Kershaw, "Key Characteristics of Japanese Mythology," History Cooperative, August 16, 2023. https://historycooperative.org.
4. Staff of Japan Today, "Why Japanese Values and Morality Confound Us So," Japan Today, October 18, 2011. https://japantoday.com.

Chapter One: The Creation of the World and Japan

5. Anonymous, Kojiki, trans. Basil H. Chamberlain. New Clarendon, VT: Tuttle, 2005, p. 22.
6. Marky Star, "Explanation of the Creation Myth," Japan This!, June 22, 2020. https://japanthis.com.
7. Star, "Explanation of the Creation Myth."
8. Joshua Frydman, *The Japanese Myths: A Guide to Gods, Heroes, and Spirits*. London: Thames and Hudson, 2022, p. 33.
9. Frydman, *The Japanese Myths*, p. 33.

Chapter Two: Tales of the Gods and Goddesses

10. Gregory Wright, "Japanese God Ebisu," Mythopedia, November 29, 2022. https://mythopedia.com.
11. Miachel Ashkenazi, *Handbook of Japanese Mythology*. Oxford, UK: ABC CLIO, 2003, p. 29.
12. Ashkenazi, *Handbook of Japanese Mythology*, p. 195.
13. Dattatreya Mandal, "12 Major Japanese Gods and Goddesses You Should Know About," Realm of History, June 16, 2023. www.realmofhistory.com.
14. Ashkenazi, *Handbook of Japanese Mythology*, p. 148.
15. Gregory Wright, "Japanese Goddess Inari," Mythopedia, December 5, 2022. https://mythopedia.com.

Chapter Three: A Host of Culture Heroes

16. Angus Sutherland, "Amakuni: Legendary Japanese Blacksmith and Father of the Samurai Sword," Ancient Pages, January 23, 2019. www.ancientpages.com.

17. Quoted in Sutherland, "Amakuni."
18. Ashkenazi, *Handbook of Japanese Mythology*, pp. 162–63.
19. Quoted in Vaughan, *Tales of Japan*, p. 31.
20. Quoted in Vaughan, *Tales of Japan*, p. 33.
21. Quoted in Vaughan, *Tales of Japan*, p. 41.
22. Yei Theodora Ozaki, *The Japanese Fairy Book*. London: Archibald Constable, 1903, pp. 65–66.
23. Frydman, *The Japanese Myths*, p. 81.

Chapter Four: Animals, Creatures, and Monsters

24. Matthew Meyer, "Uwabami," Yokai, 2024. https://yokai.com.
25. Frydman, *The Japanese Myths*, pp. 167–68.
26. Frydman, *The Japanese Myths*, p. 174.
27. Michale D. Foster, "Yokai: Fantastic Creatures of Japanese Folklore," Japan Society, 2025. https://aboutjapan.japansociety.org.

Chapter Five: Feats of the Divine Hachiman

28. Hirafuji Kikuko, "Myth and Legend: The Stories of Susanoo and Hachiman," Nippon.com, January 17, 2024. www.nippon.com.
29. Kawai Atsushi, "Saved by the Wind? The Mongol Invasions of Japan," Nippon.com, December 23, 2021. www.nippon.com.
30. Joanna Gillan, "Kamikaze: The Divine Winds That Saved Japan," Ancient Origins, April 25, 2022. www.ancient-origins.net.
31. Gillan, "Kamikaze."
32. Gillan, "Kamikaze."
33. Avid Archer, "Hachiman: God of War in Japanese Mythology," March 3, 2024. https://avid-archer.com.

Books

Reo Arashiro, *Japanese Mythology*. Self-published, 2023.

F. Hadland Davis, *Myths and Legends of Japan*. Overland Park, KS: Digrireads, 2020.

Michael D. Foster, *The Book of Yokai: Mysterious Creatures of Japanese Folklore*. Berkeley: University of California Press, 2024.

Theresa Matsurra, *The Book of Japanese Folklore*. Stoughton, MA: Adams Media, 2024.

Keisuke Nishimoto, *Strange Tales from Japan*. North Clarendon, VT: Tuttle, 2024.

F.T. Weaver, *Folktales from Japan*. Vol 1*: Timeless Stories of Courage, Magic, and Adventure for All Ages*. Self-published, 2024.

Internet Sources

D.L. Ashliman, ed., "Japanese Legends About Supernatural Sweethearts," January 1, 2015. https://sites.pitt.edu/~dash/japan love.html

Kawai Atsushi, "Saved by the Wind? The Mongol Invasions of Japan," Nippon.com, December 23, 2021. www.nippon.com.

Gabriela Baban, "Japanese Mythology: 6 Japanese Mythical Creatures," The Collector, December 28, 2021. www.thecollector.com.

Joanna Gillan, "Kamikaze: The Divine Winds That Saved Japan," Ancient Origins, April 25, 2014. www.ancient-origins.net.

Jason Hamilton, "Japanese Mythology 101: The Ultimate Guide," MythBank, December 12, 2022. https://mythbank.com.

Daniel Kershaw, "Key Characteristics of Japanese Mythology," History Cooperative, August 16, 2023. https://historycooperative .org.

Hirafuji Kikuko, "Gods Old and New: Different Types of Japanese Deities," Nippon.com, January 11, 2024. www.nippon.com.

Dattatreya Mandal, "12 Major Japanese Gods and Goddesses You Should Know About," Realm of History, June 16, 2023. www.realmof history.com.

Michaela Smith, "Japanese Mythology: Cosmogony," Michigan State University Canadian Studies, August 29, 2019. https://canadianstud ies.isp.msu.edu.

Marky Star, "Explanation of the Creation Myth," Japan This!, June 22, 2020. https://japanthis.com.

Angus Sutherland, "Amakuni: Legendary Japanese Blacksmith and Father of the Samurai Sword," Ancient Pages, January 23, 2019. www .ancientpages.com.

Gregory Wright, "Japanese Goddess Amaterasu," Mythopedia, November 29, 2022. https://mythopedia.com.

Gregory Wright, "Japanese God Tsukuyomi," Mythopedia, November 29, 2022. https://mythopedia.com.

Websites

Japanese Gods, Mythopedia
https://mythopedia.com/topics/japanese-gods
The Mythopedia website has compiled a list of most of the major Japanese gods, each with a link leading to a separate article; each article contains other links to related material.

Japanese Mythology Archive, Ancient Pages
www.ancientpages.com/category/myths-legends/japanese-mythology
The editors of the useful website Ancient Pages provide information about more than thirty characters from the Japanese myths, including gods, shape-shifters, tricksters and other strange beings, and various monsters.

Japanese Mythology, MythLok
https://mythlok.com/world-mythologies/asian/south-east-asian-mythology/japanese
This helpful site features three dozen links to separate articles about notable mythical Japanese gods, goddesses, creatures, and monsters. Each link is accompanied by a fitting, often striking painted image of the character.

Cover: D_22/Shutterstock

6: IanDagnall Computing/Alamy Stock Photo
9: The Print Collector/Heritage Images/Newscom
11: Historic Collection/Alamy Stock Photo
15: Pictures From History/Newscom
19: CPA Media Pte Ltd/Alamy Stock Photo
22: piemags/Alamy Stock Photo
26: CPA Media Pte Ltd/Alamy Stock Photo
29: Alamy Stock Photo
33: Lebrecht Music & Arts/Alamy Stock Photo
36: Pictures From History/Newscom
40: CPA Media Pte Ltd/Alamy Stock Photo
43: Science History Images/Alamy Stock Photo
45: CPA Media Pte Ltd/Alamy Stock Photo
48: Lebrecht Music & Arts/Alamy Stock Photo
51: CPA Media Pte Ltd/Alamy Stock Photo
54: Chronicle/Alamy Stock Photo

ABOUT THE AUTHOR

Classical historian and award-winning author Don Nardo has written numerous acclaimed volumes about ancient civilizations and peoples. They include more than fifty overviews of the mythologies of the Sumerians, Babylonians, Egyptians, Greeks, Romans, Persians, Celts, Hindus, Native Americans, and others. Nardo, who also composes and arranges orchestral music, lives with his wife, Christine, in Massachusetts.